# LIVING OUT OF

# LUST

FROM THE SHADOWS OF SEXUAL SIN AND INTO THE LIGHT

## HAMP LEE III

(com)mission™

PUBLISHING

MONTGOMERY, ALABAMA

# TABLE OF CONTENTS

*For this is the will of God, even your sanctification, that ye should abstain from fornication: That every one of you should know how to possess his vessel in sanctification and honour; Not in the lust of concupiscence, even as the Gentiles which know not God: That no man go beyond and defraud his brother in any matter: because that the Lord is the avenger of all such, as we also have forewarned you and testified. For God hath not called us unto uncleanness, but unto holiness.*

1 THESSALONIANS 4:3–7

# INTRODUCTION

People around the world silently live in sexual sin. Many want to live in sexual purity, but they have been unable to free themselves from its chains. Without peace or hope, they spend their lives in the shadows of fear, shame, and guilt.

I have lived in some form of sexual sin for almost my entire life. From viewing pornographic magazines and videos to having multiple relationships with women at the same time, I continually fed my sexual appetite. One magazine, video, or woman was not enough to satisfy my desires.

It was not until I confessed my faith in Jesus that I ever considered that my desires for sex, pornography, and women was wrong. Before Christ, I fed my sexual appetite without the slightest concern. But as a Christian, I learned that those actions were considered sin. And to live righteously before God, I would need to repent and turn from them, but I found it much easier to say than do.

As a married Christian, I found myself continually using pornography to feed my sexual appetite and as a coping mechanism for stress. Some days I fought off sexual temptation without a problem, and other days, I gave into it without a fight. For years, I lived in a continual cycle of temptation-sin-repentance. And though I understood God's stance on fornication, lust, and sexual sins, I returned to it like a dog returning to its vomit.[1]

Several years ago, God told me I did not have to sin sexually. By this time, I had lived with sexual sin for so long that I did not see any hope of ever being free. But God wanted me to understand that living sexually pure is possible, but it does not come without determination, vigilance, and sacrifice.

Maybe you can relate to my life of sexual sin and the struggle to abstain from it. Perhaps you are in a constant cycle of temptation-sin-repentance, or you have given up on the possibility of ever being free. If this sounds familiar, *Living Out of Lust* was written for you.

I wrote *Living Out of Lust* to share my journey toward sexual purity with you. I pray the words in this book will not only encourage you but also strengthen your resolve that living in sexual purity can become *your* reality.

---

[1] Proverbs 26:11.

# STUDY FORMATS

For many, sexual temptation and sin has been a private matter, but across the body of Christ, it affects many men and women. Based on your personal preference, you might want to read *Living Out of Lust* alone, but I would like to encourage you to study in a group setting. The encouragement, information, and support you can receive through a group study might be a great benefit for your walk in sexual purity.

*Two are better than one; because they have a good reward for their labour. For if they fall, the one will lift up his fellow: but woe to him that is alone when he falleth; for he hath not another to help him up. Again, if two lie together, then they have heat: but how can one be warm alone? And if one prevail against him, two shall withstand him; and a threefold cord is not quickly broken.* [2]

---

[2] Ecclesiastes 4:9–12.

## Personal Study

As you read each chapter at your own pace, at the end of each chapter is a *Living It Out* section with related information and questions. I highly recommend taking a few moments to answer each question, responding in a personal journal or electronic application. The goal of these questions is to help you uncover the details of your history of sexual addiction and provide plans for recovery and protection from sexual temptation and sin.

Along with the chapter readings, I have also included a thirty-five-day bible reading plan at the back of the book. The reading plan provides five devotionals for each chapter, covering additional information and perspectives to help you live in sexual purity.

### Personal Study Format

*Preparation.* Before you begin reading, have your bible, study materials, and journal or electronic application available. The journal or electronic application allows you to record your answers, thoughts, and convictions. These provide a foundation for personal and group study or review.

*Prayer.* Begin and end each study in prayer. Ask for God's help to prepare your heart and mind to hear from Him and be led into all truth.[3]

*Read.* Read the specific chapter with an open mind and heart. You do not need to answer any chapter questions after your first review. Also, take some time to review all referenced scriptures within the chapter. I recommended spending at least

---

[3] Matthew 7:7–11; John 16:13; 1 John 5:14–15.

one week or more per chapter so you might be able to meditate on the chapter contents.

*Answer.* Meditate on the chapter questions throughout the week or longer before responding. Ensure you provide honest answers to help you along your journey toward sexual purity. What you provide today will help you and many others in the years to come. If privacy is important to you, please keep your responses within secured areas or applications.

## Group Study

The second study format is the group study. As I stated earlier, *Living Out of Lust* can be hugely beneficial in group settings. Group studies are founded on godly relationships. Godly relationships are established in love[4] and built on honesty, openness, trust,[5] encouragement,[6] selflessness,[7] graceful communications,[8] and wise counsel.[9] And through these attributes, groups can experience environments where God is glorified, God's word is routinely discussed and used in practical application, godliness is encouraged and modeled, and an emphasis on walking in sexual purity is prominent.

Within the group study, each person can use the personal study format and come together on a specific day or several times throughout the week. I would like to encourage you to

---

[4] Proverbs 17:17; Matthew 22:36–40; Luke 6:31; John 13:34–35; 1 Corinthians 13:3–7; 1 John 3:18.

[5] Proverbs 16:28, 27:6; Romans 12:17; 2 Corinthians 4:1–7; Ephesians 4:25.

[6] Proverbs 27:17: Hebrews 3:12–13, 10:24–25.

[7] Romans 15:1; Philippians 2:4, 21.

[8] Ephesians 4:29, 5:4; Colossians 4:6.

[9] Proverbs 15:22, 27:9.

meet in other environments beyond studying *Living Out of Lust*. The more a group can meet and fellowship together during the week, the higher the potential to strengthen their bonds of fellowship with one another and with Christ:

*And they continued stedfastly in the apostles' doctrine and fellowship, and in breaking of bread, and in prayers. And fear came upon every soul: and many wonders and signs were done by the apostles. And all that believed were together, and had all things common; And sold their possessions and goods, and parted them to all men, as every man had need. And they, continuing daily with one accord in the temple, and breaking bread from house to house, did eat their meat with gladness and singleness of heart, Praising God, and having favour with all the people. And the Lord added to the church daily such as should be saved.*[10]

The one recurring theme in Acts 2:42-47 is togetherness. The believers studied together, fellowshipped together, ate together, prayed together, went to church together (daily), remained together, and had all things in common.

So whether you are eating together, bowling or playing cards, attending church services together, or sharing the highs and lows of life, group fellowships can help you live as a disciple and walk in sexual purity in word and deed. Each group member is strengthened and encouraged to remain committed to God as you share your life and faith with one another.

---

[10] Acts 2:42–47.

*Group Study Format*

As your group meets together to study, there are many ways you can establish meaningful conversations, exchanges, and experiences. You do not need a *formal* structure, but the following format is but one of many examples.

*Meal.* When meeting together, spend time in fellowship over a meal, beverage, or dessert. Create a relaxing atmosphere with open communication. There should be no specific boundaries on your discussions, but always be sensitive to the Spirit and your audience.

*Prayer.* As your meal concludes, begin your study in prayer. As you continue to meet, allow each person to have an opportunity to lead the group in prayer. Welcome Jesus into your study and open your hearts to the Holy Spirit.[11]

*Study.* Like the personal study format, you can choose to read the respective chapter, specific sections of the chapter, scripture references, or go directly to the chapter questions. Before, during, and after completing the chapter questions, provide opportunities for each group member to share what they learned and experienced throughout the chapter. Before concluding, summarize your comments and discussions and reinforce ways you can apply the study in your lives.

While there is a *balance* between ending a meeting on time and good dialogue that extends beyond a scheduled end time, please consider continuing your meeting. Some group members might need to work through an important revelation

---

[11] Matthew 18:20.

or conviction. Please allow these individuals to continue where time and opportunity permit.

*Prayer.* Close your study in prayer. As you conclude, ask if anyone has any specific prayer requests. While praying, incorporate elements of the chapter topic and discussions.

# THREE OBSTACLES

Sexual sin has many people feeling alone, trapped, and embarrassed. It keeps them from asking for help, no matter how badly they want it. By reading *Living Out of Lust*, you have taken a considerable step toward sexual purity, and I applaud your efforts. Before you go any further, I would like to share three *obstacles* that could keep you from experiencing all you can from this book:

*Pride*. If you allow pride to rule your life, you might deny having a problem with sexual sin. Even though you go through the same cycle of temptation-sin-repentance again and again, you might remain unaware of the destruction sexual sin creates in your life until it is too late.

*Pride goeth before destruction, and an haughty spirit before a fall.*[12]

---

[12] Proverbs 16:18.

*Fear.* People who live in sexual sin live in darkness. They hide in the shadows of fear, shame, and guilt to keep from being exposed. Fear causes them to lie, steal, cheat, and do almost anything to prevent their sinful actions from getting out. And they will remain in the darkness of sin rather than finding freedom in the light:

*For every one that doeth evil hateth the light, neither cometh to the light, lest his deeds should be reproved. But he that doeth truth cometh to the light, that his deeds may be made manifest, that they are wrought in God.*[13]

*Shame.* Shame is a companion of fear. Sexual sin often carries shameful feelings because of the disappointment and embarrassment of the acts you committed. Even when no one might know about your actions, you want to crawl under a rock. You might feel unworthy of God's forgiveness and purposefully stay away from Him—the One who can cleanse you of your sins and teach you how to live sexually pure.[14]

In addressing pride, fear, and shame, consider:

*Who you were does not have to determine who you are, and what you have done does not have to determine what you will do.* In Christ Jesus, you are not defined by what you have done. You are defined by what Jesus has done for you.[15] In Christ Jesus, you become the righteousness of God.[16] In Christ Jesus

---

[13] John 3:20–21.

[14] 1 John 1:9.

[15] Ephesians 1:7.

[16] 2 Corinthians 5:21.

you do not have to be anxious about anything. The peace of God will guard your heart and mind in Him.[17]

*As you walk after the Spirit, there is no condemnation in Christ Jesus.*[18] With condemnation comes the fear of punishment, disapproval, or criticism. There might be instances where responsibility and accountability must take place—but in Christ—there is no criticism or punishment. You are a new creature. You can walk in the newness of life and not the condemnation of your past.[19]

*Therefore if any man be in Christ, he is a new creature: old things are passed away; behold, all things are become new.*[20]

---

[17] Philippians 4:6–7.

[18] Romans 8:1.

[19] Romans 6:4; Galatians 5:16.

[20] 2 Corinthians 5:17.

*For the grace of God that bringeth salvation hath appeared to all men, Teaching us that, denying ungodliness and worldly lusts, we should live soberly, righteously, and godly, in this present world; Looking for that blessed hope, and the glorious appearing of the great God and our Saviour Jesus Christ; Who gave himself for us, that he might redeem us from all iniquity, and purify unto himself a peculiar people, zealous of good works.*

TITUS 2:11–14

# 1
# SQUARE ONE

In the first week after being baptized, a thought came to me about Satan and his knowledge of my life. I imagined him in a room filled with filing cabinets. He reached into a cabinet drawer and removed a file with my name on it. Inside the folder contained everything there was to know about me and the temptations affecting my life.

Now, I do not know if Satan has a personal file on me, but he does seem to know all about my temptations. He knows how to tempt me, when to tempt me, and who and what to use to do it.[21] And because I did not know myself or understand the methods he used, I fell for the same temptations again and again.

To combat these temptations, God wanted me to learn more about my temperament, character, and surroundings. Though these might not seem important in the area of sexual desires and lust, they were *triggers* toward sexual sin or sexual

---

[21] 1 Peter 5:8.

purity. I had to be mindful of what I saw, heard, and experienced.

Understanding myself and my life of sexual addiction has been a journey into some of the darkest areas of my life. I did not realize that as long as I kept my sexual addiction hidden, the more *life* I gave to it. And as long as I did not know myself and how I was tempted and enticed, I would remain a slave to sexual immorality. But being armed with this information could place me on the path toward sexual purity.

## Living It Out

You might have lived in sexual sin without ever considering its origin or the methods used to tempt you sexually. The road toward sexual purity begins with an inventory of who you are and the circumstances surrounding what you see, hear, and experience. Though this process might not be easy or quick, you might discover things about yourself you never knew and other things you wish you could forget.

Feelings of fear, shame, and guilt might return as you review some of the questions on the following page. The *weight* of your previous actions might be a lot to handle. Consider what I mentioned in the last section, and seek the help and support of trusted friends and family members and Christian counselors when needed.

The remainder of this chapter will provide questions to identify the origins of your sexual sin and how it has affected you since. Please answer these questions as honestly as you can. Ask the Lord to reveal the truth surrounding each one. Regardless of how long it takes or how painful it might become, remain committed to your *process* toward sexual purity.

You do not have to write down your answers if you do not feel comfortable. But I do want you to spend time meditating on each question. This might help you gain a better understanding of yourself and the sexual sins surrounding your life.

*Questions*

When were you first exposed to sexually explicit images, videos, or other sexual activity? Please describe the circumstances surrounding these initial experiences.

How have those initial experiences affected your life since?

Why do you believe you engage in sexually illicit activity today?

What patterns of sexual temptation have you discovered in your life?

What steps or actions have you taken—through the years—to overcome sexual temptation and sin?

Have you ever felt convicted or compelled to speak—or apologize—to those you might have offended or hurt because of your sexual sin? If so, why or why not? How did your conversation benefit you or them?

*Father, as these words and thoughts might bring feelings of fear, shame, and guilt, I pray You will comfort us by Your grace and Spirit. Please forgive us for the sins we have committed in Your sight. Empower us as we embark on a journey toward sexual purity and provide us with the necessary support, guidance, and relationships to lead us through our dark valleys. Bring us into pastures of freedom before Your presence. In the name of Jesus Christ, I pray. Amen.*

# 2
# STAY THAT WAY

I lived in sexual sin for so long that I thought it was impossible to live without it. I thought it was hardcoded into my DNA. I repented each time I sinned sexually, but I did not commit to a repentant lifestyle. I would soon return to my cycle of temptation-sin-repentance. So because of my struggles, I reasoned within myself that God would accept me regardless of what I was facing. I was not committing any *serious* crimes —I was a *good* person. I wanted to be obedient to God, but I was struggling to live *right*. I was doing the best I could every day. I figured I should be all right to stay the way I was.

Though I resolved within myself how I was going to live moving forward, the bible is very clear about the consequences of sexual sin.[22] I was deceiving myself and placing my eternal salvation at risk in two specific ways:

---

[22] Matthew 7:21–23; Romans 6:23; Ephesians 5:5.

*What shall we say then? Shall we continue in sin, that grace may abound? God forbid. How shall we, that are dead to sin, live any longer therein?*[23]

First, I was continuing in sin expecting for God's grace to abound toward me. I never considered that God's grace would ever run out. I figured God would always forgive, always save, and always help me—regardless of what I had done. *It is what I expected.*

The second way I placed my eternal salvation at risk was by appeasing my lustful desires. More than a decade ago, a young woman made a statement to me which I knew could lead to spending a night in a bed with her. I made the *right* decision in declining her offer, but I was so sexually *charged* that evening that I spent the next three hours viewing pornography. In those moments, I said to myself that I would rather view pornography than have sex with another woman because I would only be sinning against myself. *I made an excuse to sin.* Instead of me saying *I will not sin at all,* I said I would sin against myself and not another woman.

So when I speak about my cycle of temptation-sin-repentance, I would fight off temptation for as long as I could, then when it got too much for me to bear—which was not much—I would give into it knowing I could repent, and *I was okay.* Forgiven and cleansed.

But here was the extreme danger in my thinking. Outside of the fact that my life on the earth could end at any moment and grace was not promised to me as we find with those in Romans 1:21-32, my focus of repentance was not a dedicated commitment to walk in the newness of life or to stop serving

---

[23] Romans 6:1–2.

sin. I figured God would always forgive me no matter what I had done. I was not focused on ending a life of sin once and for all. I was comfortable remaining the way I was—living a continuous cycle of temptation-sin-repentance.

*Be not deceived; God is not mocked: for whatsoever a man soweth, that shall he also reap. For he that soweth to his flesh shall of the flesh reap corruption; but he that soweth to the Spirit shall of the Spirit reap life everlasting.*[24]

In my own life, I was sowing corruption into my flesh. And if I continued, I would reap corruption. As a disciple of Jesus, I am supposed to flee fornication altogether. But I made an excuse for it. I was sinning against my own body.[25] I sought to appease my life of sexual sin rather than committing to a life of righteousness.

*God honors free choice.* God instituted the principle of free choice from the creation of angels to man (man and woman), and He continues to honor it to this day.[26] If God wanted to control man's decisions, He would make us live holy.

*God is not going to make you stop doing anything.* God will help you, send the Holy Spirit, counsel you, provide His word, send messengers, empower you through His grace, and intercede or intervene along the way,[27] but He is not going to override His *position* of free choice. If you want to sin, God is not going to get in your way.

---

[24] Galatians 6:6-7.

[25] 1 Corinthians 6:18.

[26] Genesis 3:1–7; Isaiah 14:12–15; Revelation 12:3–9.

[27] Jonah 1–4.

*God will give you over to your sinful desires if you choose to ignore His ways.* Paul spoke to the Romans about this very issue in Romans 1:21-32. Though they knew God, they did not glorify Him as God, nor were they thankful. They became vain with their imaginations and allowed their hearts to become darkened. They exchanged the glory of the incorruptible God, changed the truth of God for a lie, served the created things more than the Creator, and exchanged natural affections for what was against nature. And because of this, God gave them up to uncleanness through the lust of their hearts, allowed them to dishonor their bodies between themselves, gave them up to vile affections that were against nature, and gave them over to a reprobate (unprincipled) mind.

If those Paul spoke about wanted to give themselves over to unnatural and sinful thoughts and actions, God was not going to stop them. He allowed them to continue down *their* road of darkened hearts, reprobate minds, and unnatural affections.

God is not going to force me to believe in Him or live by His ways. He is open to anyone willing to humble him or herself and yield to His ways, but we have to commit to the way of truth.

Being committed is a wholehearted dedication and loyalty to a cause, activity, or job. When I think about walking in the newness of life, I must be firmly committed to changing my thinking and behavior toward godliness. I cannot serve sin nor allow it to reign in my body to obey its lusts and passions.[28] I must actively work to yield myself unto God.

*Let not sin therefore reign in your mortal body, that ye should obey it in the lusts thereof. Neither yield ye your members as*

[28] Romans 6:3–14.

*instruments of unrighteousness unto sin: but yield yourselves unto God, as those that are alive from the dead, and your members as instruments of righteousness unto God. For sin shall not have dominion over you: for ye are not under the law, but under grace.*[29]

## Living It Out

Many men and women live in a continuous cycle of temptation-sin-repentance. I am not saying you or anyone else does not want to live for God, but if we think about it, we might be more committed to living for our flesh than for God. And this is a dangerous position to be in.

We must commit to walking in the newness of life in the Spirit.[30] We must maintain God's standard of holiness and not give any room to overlook, ignore, subtract, or manipulate His word or will to appease a lifestyle of sin.[31] We cannot stay in sin. We cannot remain the way we were in sexual sin. We must commit to living in righteousness.

### Questions

Have you felt you could never overcome sexual temptation and sin? Why or why not?

Have you ever overlooked, ignored, subtracted, or manipulated scriptures to appease a lifestyle of sexual sin? Please explain.

---

[29] Romans 6:12–14.

[30] Galatians 5:16–25.

[31] Revelation 22:18–19.

Review Romans 1:21-32, Galatians 5:19-21, and Galatians 6:7-8. Expound on these scriptures and consider any relevant personal stories or convictions.

If you lived in a cycle of temptation-sin-repentance, did you ever think God's grace would run out? Please explain.

Review Lamentations 3:22-23, 1 Corinthians 10:13, and Galatians 5:24. Expound on these scriptures. What declarations or commitments can you make to live in sexual purity before God?

*Father, we thank You for Your grace and patience with us. As we have sought ways to live beyond sexual sin, we have not always been successful, and sometimes chose to remain in sexual sin. Forgive us. We do not want to live in sexual sin any longer. Teach us by Your grace and Holy Spirit to be overcomers and remain faithful and committed to You and Your word. In the name of Jesus Christ, I pray. Amen.*

# 3
# CLEAN SLATE

After giving into sexual temptation, I often felt a suffocating shame and guilt.[32] I let down myself, my family and friends, and God. I wished there was somewhere I could hide from everyone, even if they did not know what I had done.

Two of the hardest things for me to accept was God forgiving me and me forgiving myself. I did not feel worthy of God's love or forgiveness. I could not understand why He would love someone who continued to give into sexual temptation time and again. I felt worthless.

In my moments of self-loathing, I leaned on my feelings and emotions of hopelessness, guilt, and shame. And because of that, I stayed away from everyone, including God. I was too ashamed to lift my head or my voice for help. I kept myself from experiencing God's grace to:

—provide unmerited favor and kindness,[33]

---

[32] Proverbs 24:10.

[33] Romans 3:24–25; Ephesians 2:8; Titus 3:4–7.

—provide a *place* to go to in my hour of greatest need,[34]

—teach me how to live in purity and righteousness,[35]

—strengthen me in my weakness.[36]

To have a clean slate from the hopelessness, guilt, and shame of sexual sin, I must repent and place my faith and trust in God. I must remove myself from the condemning thoughts and feelings that seek to keep me bound and trapped.

My heart wanted me to wallow in what I had done rather than seeking help from God because of it. My feelings and emotions wanted me focused on its need to *feel* something—often negative and sinful—rather than becoming whole and free. It was in those moments that I needed to change the foundation I stood upon. I had to live by faith and not my feelings—*faith over feelings.*

With my feelings, life seemed as if I was riding on a roller coaster. One moment I felt great, and the next moment I was sad, depressed, angry, guilt-ridden, or stressed.

The foundation of faith is in God—who He is, what He promised, and what He can—*and will*—do. Having a firm foundation in God allows me to stand against the wiles of Satan and my flesh.[37] And to cultivate my faith, I must hear God's word:

*So then faith cometh by hearing, and hearing by the word of God.*[38]

---

[34] Hebrews 4:15–16.

[35] Titus 2:11–14.

[36] 2 Corinthians 12:9–10.

[37] Ephesians 6:10-18.

[38] Romans 10:17.

God's word is quick, powerful, sharper than any two-edged sword, and never returns to Him without results.[39] And as faith comes by hearing the word of God, my mind and heart are stirred by its power. But as I hear God's word, I must also act on what I hear.[40] This is the essence of faith:

*Now faith is the substance of things hoped for, the evidence of things not seen.*[41]

In Hebrews 11:13–16, men and women died in faith, hoping for the promise of the heavenly city. The heavenly city was the *substance* they were hoping for. The *evidence* of what was not seen—*the future heavenly city*—was seen through their actions. Their actions proved what they believed.

As I apply this across God's word, what I read and hear is the *substance* of what I am hoping for—what I believe to be true. When I act on what I am hoping for, it is the *evidence* of what I believe.

I can stand on God's word instead of the roller coaster of emotions my heart and Satan wants to keep in my life. I can trust God's word and remain immovable in Him because God is greater than my heart.[42]

Each day, I must engage God's word—*by faith*. Faith reaches beyond what I see or feel.[43] Faith does not remind me of what I have done in sin but who I am in Christ. I must trust God and see myself as He sees me in repentance—redeemed

---

[39] Isaiah 55:11; Hebrews 4:12.

[40] James 1:19–25.

[41] Hebrews 11:1.

[42] 1 John 3:19–20.

[43] 2 Corinthians 5:7; Hebrews 11:1–2, 6.

through the blood of His Son and cleansed white as snow.[44] And as I keep my mind on God and His promises, I can live beyond the sting of hopelessness, guilt, shame, and condemnation:

*Thou wilt keep him in perfect peace, whose mind is stayed on thee: because he trusteth in thee.*[45]

When my mind is stayed on God through such activities as reading and studying His word, fellowship, and listening to praise and worship music, all negativity is pushed out. It gives me the opportunity to fill my mind and heart with godliness and open myself to hear from Him. It helps me understand that when I am down, God can lift me up; when I am bound, He can set me free; when I feel lonely, He never left me, and when I am in need of help, I can hold my head up and know where my help comes from.

*My help cometh from the LORD, which made heaven and earth. He will not suffer thy foot to be moved: he that keepeth thee will not slumber. Behold, he that keepeth Israel shall neither slumber nor sleep. The LORD is thy keeper: the LORD is thy shade upon thy right hand. The sun shall not smite thee by day, nor the moon by night. The LORD shall preserve thee from all evil: he shall preserve thy soul. The LORD shall preserve thy going out and thy coming in from this time forth, and even for evermore.*[46]

---

[44] Psalm 103:11–12; Isaiah 1:18; 1 John 1:5–9.

[45] Isaiah 26:3.

[46] Psalm 121.

# Living It Out

*The Lord is merciful and gracious, slow to anger, and plenteous in mercy. He will not always chide: neither will he keep his anger for ever. He hath not dealt with us after our sins; nor rewarded us according to our iniquities. For as the heaven is high above the earth, so great is his mercy toward them that fear him. As far as the east is from the west, so far hath he removed our transgressions from us.*[47]

Through Christ, you can find freedom from sexual sin and condemning thoughts and feelings of hopelessness, guilt, and shame. No matter what anyone says or believes, you can have a clean slate before God. You can come into the light and receive forgiveness and restoration.

*If we confess our sins, he is faithful and just to forgive us our sins, and to cleanse us from all unrighteousness.*[48]

*Repent.* Having a clean slate begins with coming to God and repenting of your sins. Repentance is an acknowledgment of your sins, confessing your sins to God, and a commitment to refrain from them. I pray you will make such a commitment to have a clean slate by taking a moment to repent of every sin you have committed.[49]

*Create in me a clean heart, O God; and renew a right spirit within me.*[50]

---

47 Psalm 103:8–12.

48 1 John 1:9.

49 Matthew 6:14–15; 1 John 1:9.

50 Psalm 51:10.

*Reset.* Out of the heart come such issues as sexual sin.[51] And as we turn from sexual sin, we need a clean heart and renewed spirit.

After David committed adultery with Bathsheba and had her husband killed in battle, God confronted him through Nathan the prophet.[52] David wrote a psalm about his iniquity and sin.[53] And as we repent and make a commitment to live righteously, we should also ask God to create in us a clean heart and renew a right spirit within us so we can live faithfully before God.

*Wherewithal shall a young man cleanse his way? by taking heed thereto according to thy word.*[54]

*Restore.* We maintain our way in righteousness by taking heed to God's word. To heed God's word in this sense is to guard, protect, beware, observe, watch, and preserve. This requires our active involvement in reading, studying, and meditating on God's word daily. And as we take heed to the word, we become not only hearers but doers of the word.[55]

*Questions*

*Two of the hardest things for me to accept was God forgiving me and me forgiving myself.* Have these been difficult for you as well? If so, please explain why.

---

[51] Matthew 15:18–20.

[52] 2 Samuel 11:1–12:14.

[53] Psalm 51:2.

[54] Psalm 119:9.

[55] James 1:19–25.

Do you believe you are worthy of forgiveness? Read Psalm 65:3, 80:3; Romans 10:11; 1 John 3:18–22.

Describe the ways you can keep your way pure before the Lord.

*Father, as we come to You in repentance, wash our sins away into the sea of forgetfulness. Allow us to experience Your forgiveness and the sanctifying power of Your word. Give us the courage to stand upon Your word in faith, and cast out any thoughts or feelings of doubt or worthlessness. Restore our hearts and love us abundantly through Your mercy and grace. In the name of Jesus Christ, I pray. Amen.*

# 4
# A LOST LOVE

*The reason why we engage in sexual sin, or any sin,*
*is because in those moments we do not fear or love God.*

This is a very sobering thought. To think that you do not fear or love God. If you are like me, you want to fear God. You want to love Him. You want to live in faithful obedience.

*The fear of the Lord is to hate evil: pride, and arrogancy, and the evil way, and the froward mouth, do I hate.*[56]

Fearing the Lord in this sense is having moral reverence. Moral reverence is focused on honoring and respecting God when it comes to behaviors and actions that are right, honest, just, pure, lovely, of good report, virtue, and praise.[57]

---

[56] Proverbs 8:13.

[57] Philippians 4:8.

*Thou shalt love the Lord thy God with all thy heart, and with all thy soul, and with all thy mind.*[58]

Loving God with all your heart, soul, and mind is the first and great commandment.[59] It encompasses the total and complete commitment of your life to God.

*Love.* Love is a strong feeling, affection, or personal attachment toward another person or thing. Love is also a commitment that is made by one person to another person or thing or between two people (e.g., marriage).

*Heart.* The heart is the center of your thoughts and feelings. And from out of your heart flow the issues and directions of your life.[60]

*Soul.* The soul is the breath, spirit, or life. It is the *seat* of your feelings, desires, affections, etc. The heart and mind are a part of the soul. The soul is eternal and will not end after a person's physical death.

*Mind.* The mind is the faculty of imagination and understanding. It is where deep thought is engaged.

Everything that I am, everything that is within me, and everything that I will be are given to fear and love God. And through my fear and love of God, I will turn from sexual sin and turn to Him with my all heart, soul, and mind with deep affection, commitment, and moral reverence.

---

[58] Matthew 22:37.

[59] Matthew 22:37–38.

[60] Proverbs 4:23, 27:3.

*I must fear God more than I fear pleasing my flesh.*
*I must love God more than I love myself.*

To love God with all your heart, soul, and mind will require *sacrifice*; a sacrifice of everything you once loved, desired, and sought. Such a sacrifice is a part of the *cost* that comes with being a disciple of Jesus.

*And there went great multitudes with him: and he turned, and said unto them, If any man come to me, and hate not his father, and mother, and wife, and children, and brethren, and sisters, yea, and his own life also, he cannot be my disciple. And whosoever doth not bear his cross, and come after me, cannot be my disciple. For which of you, intending to build a tower, sitteth not down first, and counteth the cost, whether he have sufficient to finish it? Lest haply, after he hath laid the foundation, and is not able to finish it, all that behold it begin to mock him, Saying, This man began to build, and was not able to finish. Or what king, going to make war against another king, sitteth not down first, and consulteth whether he be able with ten thousand to meet him that cometh against him with twenty thousand? Or else, while the other is yet a great way off, he sendeth an ambassage, and desireth conditions of peace. So likewise, whosoever he be of you that forsaketh not all that he hath, he cannot be my disciple.*[61]

Jesus said that unless we forsake *all* we have, we cannot be His disciple. *All* include television, movies, friends, career, and whatever else that might get in the way of your ability to love God and live as a faithful disciple.

---

[61] Luke 14:25–33.

A love for God increases your desire to please Him. It increases your obedience to Him.[62] A love for God solidifies your commitment and resolve to face and suffer whatever internal or external circumstance or event to remain faithful and in right standing in His presence.

## Living It Out

*Nevertheless I have somewhat against thee, because thou hast left thy first love. Remember therefore from whence thou art fallen, and repent, and do the first works; or else I will come unto thee quickly, and will remove thy candlestick out of his place, except thou repent.*[63]

The church of Ephesus was accomplishing many great things before the Lord. They had patient endurance and labored for His name's sake without ceasing. They could not bear those who were evil.[64] They even tried and discovered those who were false apostles among them.

Many of us are like those in Ephesus. We serve the Lord diligently and maintain patient endurance. We faithfully execute the will of God and perform whatever service or ministry we can. We want to be a light for God in the world.[65] We want to please God and love Him and His people. But like the people in Ephesus, God might have something *somewhat* against us.

Through our sexual sin, we might be guilty of leaving our first love—God. Though we are working, serving, and

---

[62] John 14:23.

[63] Revelation 2:4–5.

[64] Revelation 2:1.

[65] Matthew 5:14–16.

ministering in His name, in those moments of sin, our actions reveal we do not fear or love Him.

Jesus told the church of Ephesus to remember from where they fell and repent, and do the first works.[66] And before you continue to the next chapter, I want you to think about where you were. I spoke about repentance in the previous chapter, but if it is necessary now—*repent*. Return to your first works, especially the first and great commandment.[67] Spend some time—even a few days—considering the *cost* of discipleship and the sacrifice you must make to fear and love God. Choose to turn from sexual sin—and all sin—because you want to fear and love God with your all heart, mind, and soul.

Let us who have an ear, hear what the Spirit spoke to the church of Ephesus. For those who overcome, Jesus will give them fruit to eat from the tree of life, which is in the paradise of God.[68] This is the promise to those who overcome temptation and sin. I pray you will choose to overcome by fearing and loving God.

*Questions*

*The reason why we engage in sexual sin, or any sin, is because in those moments we do not fear or love God.*

Please take a few moments to summarize how the statement above has been true in your life.

What *cost* or sacrifice will you need to make to fear and love God?

---

[66] Revelation 2:5.

[67] Matthew 22:36–40.

[68] Revelation 2:7.

Read Genesis 39:1–20. How can Joseph's statement in Genesis 39:9 encourage you in your journey toward sexual purity and your relationship with God?

*Father, we thank You for Your mercies that are new every morning. We thank You for Your faithfulness and love toward us. Please forgive us for not fearing or loving You more than ourselves and our desires. We want to please You. We want to love You. We want to fear You. Help us to give ourselves in deep affection, commitment, and moral reverence in all we say and do from this moment forward. We want to live faithful lives that reflect Your love and character and bring You glory. In the name of Jesus Christ, I pray. Amen.*

# 5

# A CITY UNDER ATTACK

*He that hath no rule over his own spirit is like a city that is broken down, and without walls.*[69]

A city without walls cannot defend or protect itself from intruders, wild animals, some natural disasters, or the onslaught of an enemy. It is defenseless.

Like a city, you have internal and external *enemies* seeking to destroy you: your flesh and the devil.[70] And when you do not show self-control through fearing and loving God with your whole being, you might find yourself just as vulnerable as a broken down city without walls.

Your flesh and the devil are coming to destroy you and keep you from entering the eternal city.[71] You do not have to move far to see how they are surrounding you to break down

---

[69] Proverbs 25:28.

[70] John 10:10; 1 Peter 2:11.

[71] Hebrews 11:13–16.

your *defenses* so you might give into sexual temptation rather than endure it.

We live in a culture that promotes, enhances, and induces sexual excitement and desire. From commercials, styles and wear of clothing, television shows, and other media, we are inundated with sexual images and literature. Though they are presented as a *means* to sell merchandise or experience a level of entertainment, these images and literature do tremendous harm to our souls, not realizing the *role* they play in turning our hearts toward sexual sin.

The road to sexual sin begins long before any *event* occurs. It starts:

—at the club gym where men and women wear tight, revealing clothing,

—viewing social media, television shows, and movies with people wearing sexually explicit clothing and conducting such acts,

—with going places (even on vacation) where people wear little to no clothing.

Though you might not initially go to these *places* with the purpose of gratifying yourself sexually, you must recognize how such images and literature feed your sexual desires toward committing sexually illicit acts. To endure sexual temptation, you must build, secure, and protect yourself from such images and literature.

*Keep thy heart with all diligence; for out of it are the issues of life.*[72]

---

[72] Proverbs 4:23–27.

As the heart is the center of your thoughts and feelings, it is critical to guard your heart.[73] Solomon wrote that *above all else* to guard it.[74] And to guard your heart, you must be extremely mindful of what you see, hear, and experience.

Because I was not guarding my heart as I *experienced* the sex-driven culture around me, *seeds* of temptation planted in my heart.[75] And instead of enduring these temptations with the word of God, prayer, and being more specific about what I saw, heard, and experienced, I gave these images and literature *permission* to fill my mind and heart.

The longer I allowed sexually explicit images and literature to remain around me, the stronger its *voice* became. My desire to view more sexually explicit images and literature grew, while my love and fear of God shrank. I soon wanted to please myself more than God.

To keep my heart with all diligence and fear and love God, I will not only have to guard my heart, but I will need to restrict what I see, hear, and experience *every day, all day*. I will have to remove myself from areas with sexually explicit images and literature.

*Gyms.* As I stated earlier, club gyms are filled with people wearing tight, revealing clothing. Because my sole purpose at the gym was to work out, I was not always focused on guarding my heart. Though I was trying to keep my eyes right on and not look at women lustfully,[76] in almost every direction, there was someone dressed in tight, revealing clothing. I did not

---

[73] Proverbs 4:23, 27:3.

[74] Ibid.

[75] James 1:13–15.

[76] Proverbs 4:25.

realize how these *encounters* were slowly moving me closer and closer to sexual sin. So to better guard my heart and life, I canceled my membership and purchased a home gym.

*Social media.* Within social media sources, I reduced my viewing *footprint.* Where there were people who often wore tight, revealing clothing or provided such images on their news feed, I either stopped following them or removed them from my account.

*Media.* I almost entirely stopped watching television shows and movies because of their emphasis to highlight and promote worldliness and sex.

*Vacations.* Like club gyms, some locations are filled with women wearing tight, revealing clothing. There are some places I will no longer travel for *rest* because that is not all that awaits me in those areas.

When many people think about what they might have to sacrifice and restrict from their lives, they think of it in terms of what they are *losing*:

—television shows they like,
—movies they want to see,
—places they want to travel,
—people they want to see.

I will not say that I did not want to watch certain shows or go to specific locations because I did. But I soon learned that this is a part of the *cost—the sacrifice—*that comes with being a disciple of Jesus.[77] And if I wanted to remain as a city on a hill

---

[77] Luke 14:25–33.

that shines its light to bring glory to God, it will be worth everything I give up.[78] An eternity with God is priceless.

*Thy word have I hid in mine heart, that I might not sin against thee.[79]*

David hid God's word in his heart so he would not sin against Him. God's word became so deeply ingrained in his heart that it shaped his character and steered the direction of his life toward righteousness.

Hiding God's word in your heart is a practice of active engagement. It encompasses a process of meditating on His word.[80] Meditation is an experience of imagining, muttering, speaking, studying, and talking about God's word. It is an all-day commitment of engaging His word to shape your heart and life in holiness.

If we come back to the idea of sacrifice and cost, to hide God's word in your heart might require a sacrifice of watching television or some other hobby you typically invest in. Meditation is an experience of giving as much of your day as possible to imagining, muttering, speaking, studying, and talking about God's word.

*Be sober, be vigilant; because your adversary the devil, as a roaring lion, walketh about, seeking whom he may devour: Whom resist stedfast in the faith, knowing that the same afflictions are accomplished in your brethren that are in the world. But the God of all grace, who hath called us unto his*

---

[78] Matthew 5:14–16.

[79] Psalm 119:11.

[80] Joshua 1:1–8.

*eternal glory by Christ Jesus, after that ye have suffered a while, make you perfect, stablish, strengthen, settle you.*[81]

The devil is roaming about, looking for people. He is looking at all *cities*, trying to find vulnerabilities or create ways to bring down their defenses and devour them. He has been doing this with you and me through sexual temptation and sin, among other things. But we can protect ourselves against the onslaught of the devil. Peter speaks of four things we can do in 1 Peter 5:8–10:

*Be sober.* To be sober is to be calm and collected in spirit, temperate, rational, and circumspect.[82] It is different from being emotional or irrational. Like a person who becomes drunk and loses his or her inhibitions to make intelligent choices or decisions, so is someone who is emotional or irrational. The devil and your flesh will try to leverage what you see, hear, and experience to *trigger* self-gratifying responses to sexual temptation.

*Be vigilant.* Being vigilant will require you to be watchful, focused, and attentive to what you see, hear, and experience. Sexual temptation can occur anywhere, at any time, and without notice. Satan and your flesh do not take coffee breaks and will not care if you had a long day at work. Whether it is six o'clock in the morning or ten o'clock at night, you must be

---

[81] 1 Peter 5:8–10.

[82] Blue Letter Bible. "Dictionary and Word Search for nēphō (Strong's 3525)." Blue Letter Bible. 1996–2013. 27 May 2013. http://www.blueletterbible.org/lang/lexicon/lexicon.cfm?Strongs=G3525&t=KJV.

ready to defend the boundaries of your mind and heart with discipline and self-control.[83]

*Resist steadfast in the faith.* Let's break down the words resist, steadfast, and faith, and then bring them back together. To resist is to set yourself against, to withstand, and oppose.[84] Steadfast is something that is strong, firm, immovable, solid, hard, and rigid.[85] Faith is the conviction of man's relationship to God and divine things; the conviction that God exists and is the creator and ruler of all things, the provider, and bestower of eternal salvation through Jesus Christ; and a strong conviction that Jesus is the Messiah, through whom we obtain eternal salvation in the kingdom of God.[86] Understanding these definitions, you must be rigid and immovable against the onslaught of temptation because of your conviction of God, your faithful and obedient relationship with Him, and the eternal salvation which comes through Jesus Christ.

*Endure suffering.* There were many times when sexual temptation seemed so intense that my body ached for sexual pleasure. I felt like I was going to die if I did not give into it. In those moments, I was not sober, vigilant, or resisting steadfast in the faith. I was thinking about how I could satisfy my sexual

---

[83] Galatians 6:9; Ephesians 4:27.

[84] Blue Letter Bible. "Dictionary and Word Search for anthistēmi (Strong's 436)." Blue Letter Bible. 1996–2013. 27 May 2013. http://www.blueletterbible.org/lang/lexicon/lexicon.cfm?Strongs=G436&t=KJV.

[85] Blue Letter Bible. "Dictionary and Word Search for stereos (Strong's 4731)." Blue Letter Bible. 1996–2013. 27 May 2013. http://www.blueletterbible.org/lang/lexicon/lexicon.cfm?Strongs=G4731&t=KJV.

[86] Blue Letter Bible. "Dictionary and Word Search for pistis (Strong's 4102)." Blue Letter Bible. 1996–2013. 28 May 2013. http://www.blueletterbible.org/lang/lexicon/lexicon.cfm?Strongs=G4102&t=KJV.

desires above pleasing God. And after reaching that point, it was not too long before I gave into my lustful desires. But I had to learn how to endure the temptations which war against my mind and flesh.

*There hath no temptation taken you but such as is common to man: but God is faithful, who will not suffer you to be tempted above that ye are able; but will with the temptation also make a way to escape, that ye may be able to bear it.*[87]

1. *There is no temptation that is not common to man.* Many people facing sexual temptation and sin often feel as if they are the only person in the world dealing with it. But you are not alone. Feeling as if you are alone isolates you from others, often in fear of being exposed. And this is precisely where your flesh and the devil want you—alone, afraid, and unwilling to seek help. But your freedom comes when you are willing to walk into the light and seek help from God and others.[88]

2. *God is faithful.* This is a comforting assurance that even in the midst of your temptations, God is faithful to save, faithful to help, and faithful to His word. God does not lie, and He is willing to help you.[89]

3. *God will not allow you to be tempted above what you are able.* Regardless of how much or how strong any temptation might seem, God will not allow you to face something you are incapable of handling.

---

[87] 1 Corinthians 10:13.

[88] John 3:19–21; James 5:16.

[89] Numbers 23:19; Matthew 11:28–30; 1 John 1:9.

4. *God will make a way to escape from temptation so you will be able to bear it.* God will provide a way for you to escape temptation. As God will not lead you into temptation, I want you to understand—*very clearly*—that you are not guaranteed to live a temptation-free life from this point forward.[90] God will make a way for you to escape temptation so you can bear it. Being exposed to sexual temptation does not cause you to sin—acting on the temptation does. *Walking in sexual purity is not in the absence of sexual temptations, it is in spite of it.*

The purpose for making a way for you to escape temptation is so you can bear it. To bear something is to undergo hardship and endure—weather or withstand.[91] God makes a way for you to escape from temptation to patiently endure it. And when you endure temptation, you become perfect and entire, wanting nothing:

*My brethren, count it all joy when ye fall into divers temptations; Knowing this, that the trying of your faith worketh patience. But let patience have her perfect work, that ye may be perfect and entire, wanting nothing.[92]*

There are many ways God can make—or provide—a way of escape. In the midst of sexual temptation, I have heard God tell me to call my wife, leave the house, look away, turn off the computer, go another direction, or end a conversation.

---

[90] Matthew 6:13.

[91] Blue Letter Bible. "Dictionary and Word Search for hypopherō (Strong's 5297)." Blue Letter Bible. 1996–2013. 28 May 2013. http://www.blueletterbible. org/lang/lexicon/lexicon.cfm?Strongs=G5297&t=KJV.

[92] James 1:2–4.

With each temptation you face, you will need to endure it with vigilance while resisting steadfast in the faith. When you do this, Peter outlines four things from 1 Peter 5:8–10 that Jesus will accomplish on your behalf toward holiness unto God:[93]

*Make you perfect.* One of the definitions of *perfect* is to make one what he ought to be.[94] Being in Jesus Christ will teach, mold, and shape you into perfection, conforming you to His image.[95] Through your obedience to His commands and ways, you are being prepared for eternal life through righteousness and holiness, without any blemishes of sin.[96] And one day, you will dwell in the eternal city, where God will be with you and be your God. He will wipe away your tears, and you will never experience death, sorrow, crying, or pain again.[97]

*Establish you.* To establish something is to make it stable, place firmly, or set fast or fixed.[98] Your *position* of perfection and standing in Christ will be firmly secured as you submit yourself unto God.[99]

*Strengthen you.* When you are strengthened, you are empowered through the grace of God in knowledge, patient

---

[93] Hebrews 12:14.

[94] Blue Letter Bible. "Dictionary and Word Search for katartizō (Strong's 2675)." Blue Letter Bible. 1996–2013. 14 Jun 2013. http://www.blueletterbible.org/lang/lexicon/lexicon.cfm?Strongs=G2675&t=KJV.

[95] Romans 8:28–29; Colossians 1:27–28.

[96] Matthew 28:18–20; Ephesians 5:23–27; Hebrews 12:5–14.

[97] 1 Corinthians 15:35–49; Revelation 21:3–5.

[98] Blue Letter Bible. "Dictionary and Word Search for stērizō (Strong's 4741)." Blue Letter Bible. 1996–2013. 2 Jul 2013. http://www.blueletterbible.org/lang/lexicon/lexicon.cfm?Strongs=G4741&t=KJV.

[99] Psalm 1:1–3; John 10:27–30; James 4:7–10.

endurance, deep love, and walking in the Spirit.[100] God's grace will teach you how to deny ungodliness and worldly lusts so you might live soberly, righteously, and godly.[101]

*Settle you.* To settle something is to lay the foundation or to make stable or establish.[102] When you are settled in Christ, the onslaught of your flesh or the devil will not be able to move you from your *place* in Him. Your *city* will remain protected and secure—not saying attacks will not come—but you will be able to endure each one.

## Living It Out

Paul wrote to the Ephesians not to give place to the devil.[103] This *place* is any portion or space marked off or an opportunity or occasion for action.[104] If you give your flesh or the devil a *place* in your thoughts and hearts, you allow them direct access to tempt you further toward sexual sin. But to live in sexual purity, you must take an active approach.

Taking an active stance against sexual temptation and sin is a crucial step for living sexually pure. Make sure you are active and watchful while being sober, vigilant, steadfast in the faith, and while enduring suffering.

---

[100] Galatians 5:16–26.

[101] Titus 2:11–12.

[102] Blue Letter Bible. "Dictionary and Word Search for themelioō (Strong's 2311)." Blue Letter Bible. 1996–2013. 2 Jul 2013. http://www.blueletterbible.org/lang/lexicon/lexicon.cfm?Strongs=G2311&t=KJV.

[103] Ephesians 4:27.

[104] Blue Letter Bible. "Dictionary and Word Search for topos (Strong's 5117)." Blue Letter Bible. 1996–2013. 2 Jul 2013. http://www.blueletterbible.org/lang/lexicon/lexicon.cfm?Strongs=G5117&t=KJV.

*Questions*

Do you typically address tempting situations you see, hear, or experience immediately? Why or why not?

How can entertainment sources such as television, movies, and music increase desires toward sexually illicit activity?

How can Psalm 1:1–3 help you to stay clear of sexually tempting thoughts, people, and situations?

*Father, we ask for Your help in taking an active stance against sexual temptation and sin. Forgive us for not being focused, aware, or obedient to Your word in our moments of temptation. We thank You for Your continued love and patience as we are cleansed and perfected by Your love, grace, and the blood of Your Son Jesus. Empower us with the strength we need to continue fighting the good fight of faith until the day of Jesus Christ. In the name of Jesus Christ, I pray. Amen.*

# 6
# BODYBUILDING

*For bodily exercise profiteth little: but godliness is profitable unto all things, having promise of the life that now is, and of that which is to come.[105]*

As you guard your heart with all diligence, it will be important to build up your body. Building your body in this sense is not for exercise but to walk in godliness. You ensure that along with your heart, your eyes, ears, mouth, feet, and hands will help you remain sexually pure.

*Eyes.[106]*

*The light of the body is the eye: if therefore thine eye be single, thy whole body shall be full of light. But if thine eye be evil, thy whole body shall be full of darkness. If therefore the light that is in thee be darkness, how great is that darkness![107]*

---

[105] 1 Timothy 4:8.

[106] 2 Samuel 11; Psalm 101:3; Matthew 6:22–23.

[107] Proverbs 6:25; Matthew 5:27–28, 6:22–23.

Your eyes are the receptors for the world around you. Based on what you see, your mind is fed with information and thoughts and imaginations are produced in your heart, your senses are heightened, and feelings and emotions become engaged.

Growing up, I had a habit of *scanning* women. If a woman walked past me, I would take a moment or two to look up and down her body. I also found myself *scanning* women through social media. I would view the social media pages of women I knew (and others) who wore tight, revealing clothing. Though looking at women in this manner seemed as *natural* as breathing, it was feeding my sexual desires toward sin.[108]

It took me a long time to get out of the habit of looking at women up and down their bodies—in person and on social media. I had to become more aware of who and what was around me and what I was watching. I had to keep my eyes straight ahead and remain vigilant, mentally engaged, and focused.

*Let thine eyes look right on, and let thine eyelids look straight before thee.*[109]

In addition to addressing what I was viewing, I also had to change my perception of women:

*Rebuke not an elder, but intreat him as a father; and the younger men as brethren; The elder women as mothers; the younger as sisters, with all purity.*[110]

---

[108] James 1:13–15.

[109] Proverbs 4:25.

[110] 1 Timothy 5:1–2.

Over the years, I considered women as *objects* for sexual desire and pleasure rather than pillars of virtue, respect, and grace. I had to reconcile my sinful thoughts and feelings to see women not as a means to gratify sexual desires but as mothers and sisters—relationships of honor, respect, appreciation, and support.

*Mind.*[111]

*Thou wilt keep him in perfect peace, whose mind is stayed on thee: because he trusteth in thee.*[112]

The battle for your soul begins in your mind. You are what you think.[113] If you keep your mind on the Lord and living sexually pure, you will not think about sexually explicit images or behaviors.[114]

*Wherefore gird up the loins of your mind, be sober, and hope to the end for the grace that is to be brought unto you at the revelation of Jesus Christ; As obedient children, not fashioning yourselves according to the former lusts in your ignorance: But as he which hath called you is holy, so be ye holy in all manner of conversation; Because it is written, Be ye holy; for I am holy.*[115]

To live in sexual purity, you must gird up the loins of your mind. Think of your mind as a pair of sneakers. Unlaced

---

[111] Matthew 18:18; Romans 12:1–2; Ephesians 4:17–19.

[112] Isaiah 26:3.

[113] Proverbs 23:7.

[114] Isaiah 26:3.

[115] 1 Peter 1:13–16.

sneakers can be a hazard for tripping, falling, or becoming unbalanced. In the same manner, an *unlaced* mind can welcome all types of sinful thoughts and destructive behaviors.

*Casting down imaginations, and every high thing that exalteth itself against the knowledge of God, and bringing into captivity every thought to the obedience of Christ*[116]

To keep the loins of your mind girded, it is crucial to cast down imaginations and every high thing that exalts itself against the knowledge of God. Things that seek to promote themselves against the knowledge of God are ungodly and worldly. They are not always blatantly obvious—but at their core—they can turn you away from the way and will of God. It is in these moments that you must make the conscious decision to keep your mind on God and thoughts that are true, honest, lovely, of good report, virtue, and praise.

*Finally, brethren, whatsoever things are true, whatsoever things are honest, whatsoever things are just, whatsoever things are pure, whatsoever things are lovely, whatsoever things are of good report; if there be any virtue, and if there be any praise, think on these things.*[117]

*Ears.*

*Bow down thine ear, and hear the words of the wise, and apply thine heart unto my knowledge. For it is a pleasant thing if thou keep them within thee; they shall withal be fitted in thy lips.*[118]

---

[116] 2 Corinthians 10:5.

[117] Philippians 4:8.

[118] Proverbs 22:17–18.

To bow down your ear is to listen carefully. This is an intentional act to hear the words of the wise. The words of the wise can keep you encouraged, motivated, and focused. They help you remain steady on the path of righteousness, sexual purity, and success.

*Mouth.*[119]

*Let your speech be alway with grace, seasoned with salt, that ye may know how ye ought to answer every man.*[120]

What you speak is a culmination of what is in your mind and heart. With your mouth, you can build up or tear down or encourage or discourage.[121] Choose to answer every man with grace, wisdom, and kindness.[122]

*Feet.*

*Flee from youthful lusts; but pursue righteousness, faith, love, and peace with those who call on the Lord out of a pure heart.*[123]

In 2 Timothy 16–22, Paul spoke of vain babblings that increased more ungodliness and the cankerous work of Hymenaeus and Philetus. He said they had erred in their *truth* by announcing the resurrection of Jesus had already past, overthrowing the faith of some. Paul went on to say that men should purge themselves from things that lead to dishonor and

---

119 Psalm 17:3, 19:3; Proverbs 10:11, 32, 13:3, 16:23, 18:4, 21:33; Ecclesiastes 5:2–3; Matthew 12:34; Ephesians 4:29.

120 Colossians 4:6.

121 1 Corinthians 15:55.

122 Psalm 37:30; Proverbs 18:4

123 2 Timothy 2:22.

be a vessel of honor—sanctified, ready for the Master's use, and prepared for every good work.[124]

Verse 22 deals with the approach Timothy was to take within himself and the company he kept. In the context of sexual temptation and addressing youthful lusts, there are two ways you can flee from them.

The first way you can flee from youthful lusts is to depart from them physically. When writing to his son, Solomon warned him to remove himself far from a strange woman and not to go near her door.[125] There are some people and places that increase sexual desire within you. Some are more obvious than others. Sure, the building with the flashing XXX sign is one, but other situations are as unassuming as a residential home of a close friend.

Some people might deceive themselves into believing they are *strong* enough to remain in questionable (tempting) situations. Others view running away as a sign of weakness rather than a sign of wisdom and strength. *You do not have to prove you are strong enough to fight off sexual temptation!* The longer you choose to remain around sexually tempting situations, the weaker your resolve might become to refrain from them.

The second way you can flee from youthful lusts is by restricting your access to sexually explicit media. As I stated earlier, these *outlets*—such as television and movies—often provide sexual images and literature where your imagination might run *wild*, feeding your fleshly desires. So if you know you struggle with pornography, watching half-naked men or women on television or in movies will not help you live holy

---

[124] 2 Timothy 2:21.

[125] Proverbs 5:3–13.

unto God. Those images can feed your thoughts, fill your heart, and grow until they give birth to sin.[126]

You will need to make conscious decisions about the media you choose to watch—if at all. Much of what comes from media sources are filled with ungodliness and worldliness—the lust of the eyes and flesh and the pride of life.[127]

In fleeing youthful lusts, Paul mentioned four things for Timothy to pursue. He encouraged Timothy to pursue righteousness, faith, love, and peace with those who call on the Lord out of a pure heart. This is an intentional act to earnestly endeavor or run to acquire righteousness, faith, love, and peace. For us, pursuing sexual purity must be a deliberate decision.

*Ponder the path of thy feet, and let all thy ways be established. Turn not to the right hand nor to the left: remove thy foot from evil.*[128]

*Hands.*

*Who shall ascend into the hill of the Lord? or who shall stand in his holy place? He that hath clean hands, and a pure heart; who hath not lifted up his soul unto vanity, nor sworn deceitfully. He shall receive the blessing from the Lord, and righteousness from the God of his salvation. This is the generation of them that seek him, that seek thy face, O Jacob. Selah.*[129]

---

[126] James 1:13–15.

[127] 1 John 2:15–17.

[128] Proverbs 4:26–27.

[129] Psalm 24:3–6.

Those who will be able to ascend to the hill of the Lord and stand in His holy place accomplish four things. They 1) have clean hands, 2) a pure heart, 3) have not lifted his soul unto vanity, 4) and have not sworn deceitfully. Having clean hands represent actions that are innocent, blameless, and guiltless.

As your hands complete the actions of your mind and heart, your hands will not touch or do anything you do not want to. Therefore, it will be important to have the other areas of your life in *check* to keep your hands clean before God.

## Living It Out

*Put away from thee a froward mouth, and perverse lips put far from thee. Let thine eyes look right on, and let thine eyelids look straight before thee. Ponder the path of thy feet, and let all thy ways be established. Turn not to the right hand nor to the left: remove thy foot from evil.*[130]

In what specific ways can you protect your eyes, mind, ears, heart, mouth, feet, and hands from sexual temptation and sin?

*Father, we thank You for creating us in Your image. The beauty and intricacy of our creation are wonderful. We ask for Your help in molding our eyes, mind, ears, heart, mouth, feet, and hands in sole dedication to You and Your purposes. Cleanse our hearts and allow us to be used as vessels unto honor, sanctified and prepared for Your use and every good work. In the name of Jesus Christ, I pray. Amen.*

---

[130] Proverbs 4:23–27.

# 7

# MILITARY SUPPORT

Military organizations around the world have armories to store their weapons. These organizations use armories to support military operations, defend their organization's interests, or directly engage their adversary. As adversaries to sexual purity, your flesh and the devil fight for control of your heart, soul, and mind. Therefore, it will be vital for you to build an armory to help you live righteously before God.

*Finally, my brethren, be strong in the Lord, and in the power of his might. Put on the whole armour of God, that ye may be able to stand against the wiles of the devil. For we wrestle not against flesh and blood, but against principalities, against powers, against the rulers of the darkness of this world, against spiritual wickedness in high places. Wherefore take unto you the whole armour of God, that ye may be able to withstand in the evil day, and having done all, to stand. Stand therefore, having your loins girt about with truth, and having on the breastplate of righteousness; And your feet shod with the preparation of the gospel of peace; Above all, taking the shield of faith, wherewith ye shall be able to quench all the fiery darts of the wicked. And take the helmet of salvation, and the sword of the Spirit, which is the word*[131]

*Truth.* Truth is opposed to falsehood, is honorable, upright, and not lacking in integrity.[132] *What a great place to have truth!* With your loins fastened with truth, you do not seek to gratify any lustful desires. Your desire is to live with honor and integrity among your fellow man and before God. You will live unashamed in the light rather than hiding in the darkness of lies and deceit from sexual sin.[133]

*Breastplate of Righteousness.* A breastplate is a piece of armor that covers one of the most important organs in your body—the heart. This breastplate is in right standing with God—morally upright and without guilt or sin. You put on the breastplate of righteousness to shield your heart against the onslaught of your flesh and the devil and his forces.[134] The breastplate of righteousness can keep your heart clean, upright, and undefiled before God.[135]

*Gospel of Peace.* Your feet will be fitted in preparation to take action and progress the Gospel message: sharing the life, teachings, death, resurrection, and return of Jesus Christ. The Gospel also keeps you grounded, firm, and secure in Jesus.[136]

---

[131] Ephesians 6:10–17.

[132] Proverbs 12:17, 19.

[133] John 3:19–21.

[134] Proverbs 4:23; Mark 7:1–23.

[135] Psalm 37:30–31, 40:8, 51:10, 86:11, 119:11, 111–112; Proverbs 2:10–12, 3:3–6, 4:23, 14:30; Titus 1:15; 1 John 3:19–20

[136] Matthew 13:18–23; Acts 4:12; 1 Corinthians 3:11.

*Shield of Faith.* A shield is a broad piece of armor made of rigid material and strapped to the arm or carried in hand for protection against hurled weapons. This shield carries the unwavering belief that Jesus is the Son of God and promised Messiah. And through your belief and hope in Him, eternal salvation exists.

Through faith, you can extinguish *all* of the fiery darts of the wicked. These fiery darts can be as simple as a single thought or action. But if left unprotected or unchecked, these darts will spread like wildfire in your mind and heart to overwhelm you into fear and submission toward sin and disobedience to God.

*Helmet of Salvation.* A helmet is a piece of armor, usually made of metal, designed to protect the head. The helmet of salvation keeps your thoughts and mind secure in the hope you have in Jesus Christ. As the most significant battle for your soul begins in your mind, it is vital for you to live by faith and the hope of eternal life to come.[137]

*Sword of the Spirit.* As the word of God, use the Sword of the Spirit when your flesh and the devil are on the attack to tempt you into sin.[138] The Sword of the Spirit can also be used to protect your mind, heart, and actions. But you must be willing to wield it through seasons of practice and training.[139]

---

[137] Hebrews 11:6, 13–16.

[138] Matthew 4:1–11.

[139] 1 Corinthians 9:24–27; 2 Timothy 2:5, 3:16–17, 4:1–5; Hebrews 5:14.

*Additional weapons.* Beyond the whole armor of God, include the use of website blockers, accountability software, support groups, books, etc. to remain sexually pure.

*No matter how extensive your armory might be, it is no good if you never use it.*

## Living It Out

Explain how using the full armor of God can help you live in sexual purity.

Outside of the full armor of God, what other items can you place in your armory to help you remain sexually pure?

*Father, we thank You for giving us the full armor of God to help us stand against the wiles of our flesh and the devil. May we always be equipped and ready to defend the borders of our hearts, souls, and minds in righteousness. In the name of Jesus Christ, I pray. Amen.*

# CONCLUSION

*Blessed is the man that endureth temptation: for when he is tried, he shall receive the crown of life, which the Lord hath promised to them that love him.*[140]

The crown of life. It is the hope for those who love the Lord. And to receive this crown, you must endure the temptations that come into your life.

I pray the information within this book has been a blessing to you. I pray you have been challenged, encouraged, and motivated to live a sexually pure life before God.

You do not have to remain in the shadows of shame, fear, and guilt. You can live without sinning sexually. *You do not have to sin.*

May your journey in sexual purity before God please His heart and inspire others around you to come out of the shadows of sexual sin and into the light. God bless.

---

[140] James 1:12.

# BIBLE READING PLAN

The following thirty-five-day bible reading plan is an additional resource you can use as you read through *Living Out of Lust*. Each devotional covers additional information and perspectives from the corresponding chapter, Monday–Friday. Please use Saturday and Sunday as catchup days or to reflect on your previous readings.

Week 1—Days 1–5—Square One

Week 2—Days 6–10—Stay That Way

Week 3—Days 11–15—Clean Slate

Week 4—Days 16–20—A Lost Love

Week 5—Days 21–25—A City Under Attack

Week 6—Days 26–30—Bodybuilding

Week 7—Days 31–35—Military Support

## Square One

### DAY 1

1 Thessalonians 4:3–7—*For this is the will of God, even your sanctification, that ye should abstain from fornication: That every one of you should know how to possess his vessel in sanctification and honour; Not in the lust of concupiscence, even as the Gentiles which know not God: That no man go beyond and defraud his brother in any matter: because that the Lord is the avenger of all such, as we also have forewarned you and testified. For God hath not called us unto uncleanness, but unto holiness.*

It is the will of God that we abstain from fornication. But many of us live without ever knowing how to possess our bodies in sanctification and honor. And though it seems we take one step forward and two back, the reality is that many people had come before us and overcome sexual sin. We too can overcome.

I would like to believe that no one comes to God wanting to remain in sexual sin. Many of us have not learned how to live any other way or are struggling to use the tools given to us.

As God is calling you to holiness today, I pray this is the first step in a lifelong journey of sexual purity. Take a few moments to consider what overcoming sexual sin means for you and those you love.

DAY 2

Proverbs 26:11—*As a dog returneth to his vomit, so a fool returneth to his folly.*

The thought of a dog returning to his vomit is pretty disgusting. The dog is trying to eat again what its body rejected.

As nasty as it is to read this, consider your return to sexual sin in the same manner. God wants you to reject sin and turn from it, but you return to it again and again.

You were not created to sin sexually. You were created to glorify God.[141] The *worth* you see in sexual sin has no real value because it leads to death.[142] But each time it was presented before you—via temptation—you forgot about its worthlessness or danger to your body and soul.

No matter how many times a dog returns to its vomit, the outcome will be the same. And if we continue to return to sexual sin, our outcome might end in death.[143] Let this day be one where you refuse to return to sexual sin.

---

[141] Isaiah 43:7.

[142] Romans 6:23.

[143] Revelation 21:8.

## DAY 3

John 3:20–21—*For every one that doeth evil hateth the light, neither cometh to the light, lest his deeds should be reproved. But he that doeth truth cometh to the light, that his deeds may be made manifest, that they are wrought in God.*

Many people who engage in sexual immorality work hard to keep it hidden. They do not want to be exposed because they are fearful of the outcome.

Though there might be some *losses* as we accept accountability for our actions, hopelessness, shame, and guilt do not linger. There is no condemnation for those who are in Christ Jesus.[144] We are free and can walk unashamed in the light. We no longer need to fear being exposed or worry about our future...*we have nothing to hide!*

It is a blessed feeling not to worry about who knows what you are doing. You can rest peacefully knowing that your works are originated from God and not yourself or any sin.

*Choose this day to come into the light.*

*Live in freedom.*

*Walk in peace.*

---

[144] Romans 8:1.

DAY 4

1 John 1:9—*If we confess our sins, he is faithful and just to forgive us our sins, and to cleanse us from all unrighteousness.*

Coming into the light begins with repentance. Repentance is an acknowledgment of your sins, confessing your sins to God, and a commitment to refrain from them.

God is faithful and just to forgive you of your sins. He is patient with you and longs for you to repent.[145] It is not His will for you or anyone else to perish.

Take some time to confess your sins unto God—all of them. God will cleanse you from all your unrighteousness. And as you face times of temptation or weakness, ask for His grace so His power can help you live as a faithful witness unto Him and those around you.[146]

---

[145] 2 Peter 3:9.

[146] 1 Corinthians 10:13; 2 Corinthians 12:7–10.

## DAY 5

Ecclesiastes 4:10–12—*For if they fall, one will lift up his fellow. But woe to him who is alone when he falls and has not another to lift him up! Again, if two lie together, they keep warm, but how can one keep warm alone? And though a man might prevail against one who is alone, two will withstand him—a threefold cord is not quickly broken.*

Having good friends, mentors, and leaders in your life can be invaluable for living in sexual purity. They call to check on you or invite you over to help you remain focused on God. Thank God for them.

Consider the friends, mentors, and leaders you have in your life. Thank them for their selfless giving in helping you on your journey toward sexual purity.

*If you have yet to develop such connections, ask God to bring these types of people into your life.*

## Stay That Way

DAY 6

Romans 6:23—*For the wages of sin is death; but the gift of God is eternal life through Jesus Christ our Lord.*

There is no sugar coating here. The payment for sin is death. It is a sobering truth, and one many of us do not want to come to terms with. We want to think about our lives of sexual sin as everything but sin. We call it by many other names, but in the end, it is sin.

I know you do not want to experience this death, and neither do I. But often, this is not on our minds when we think about sexual sin. We are focused on self-gratification. We do not see the destruction and pain sin causes our lives and those connected to us. We do not see how sexual sin can impact the generations of children who come behind us.

See, *death* is not only coming for you. It wants everyone and everything connected to you. Remaining in sexual sin and giving an excuse for it is death: death for you and possibly death for many others. Choose this day to accept the gift of forgiveness through Jesus Christ. Allow Him to forgive you of your sins and cleanse you from all unrighteousness.[147]

---

[147] 1 John 1:9.

## DAY 7

*Psalm* 139:7—*Whither shall I go from thy spirit? or whither shall I flee from thy presence?*

Many of us had sought to engage in sexual sin when no one was home, late at night, or even in another city where no one knew us. But no matter how far you travel or what time of the day or night it is, God sees you.

Reading through Psalm 139, David describes how there is nowhere he can go from the Lord's presence. The Lord is in the highest of heavens and the deepest parts of the earth.

I pray knowing God is always watching will convict you to display a life of purity and faith in His presence.

## DAY 8

2 Peter 3:9—*The Lord is not slack concerning his promise, as some men count slackness; but is longsuffering to us–ward, not willing that any should perish, but that all should come to repentance.*

God is all-knowing, all-powerful, and is everywhere. Nothing is impossible for Him. But God is also long-suffering. His purpose in long-suffering is to give us time to come to repentance.

It is not God's desire for any of us to perish. He created us for His glory, and He wants to spend an eternity with us. God is showing us mercy today. He is revealing His kindness. God is providing us with every opportunity to overcome sexual sin and live for Him.

## DAY 9

Romans 6:1–2—*What shall we say then? Shall we continue in sin, that grace may abound? God forbid. How shall we, that are dead to sin, live any longer therein?*

God is gracious. And because of His grace, many of us do not see an immediate response—or punishment—to our sexual sin. It seems like we have gotten away with something—giving us the *courage* to remain in it. A *little* here sin, and a *bit* there. Nothing happens. We experience His goodness in spite of our behaviors of sexual sin.[148]

Grace is not a means—or reason—to continue sinning. As you have learned, God sees all and the payment for sin is death. And even when we might not *deserve* any better, God displays His kindness and grace once again.

But please do not think for one moment that you have gotten away with anything. If you read Matthew 7:21–23, there will be many who will call on the Lord on the last day, and have done great works, but will not be able to enter into the kingdom of God. Their actions did not provide them *entry* as they thought because God was looking for their obedience, which they ignored.

God's grace is sufficient, and His power is made perfect in our weakness,[149] but it is not a license for us to continue in sexual sin. May His grace strengthen us in our weak and struggling areas so we can remain dead to sin.

---

[148] Luke 6:35.

[149] 2 Corinthians 12:9–10.

## DAY 10

Romans 1:21–32—*Professing themselves to be wise, they became fools, And changed the glory of the uncorruptible God into an image made like to corruptible man, and to birds, and fourfooted beasts, and creeping things. Wherefore God also gave them up to uncleanness through the lusts of their own hearts, to dishonour their own bodies between themselves: Who changed the truth of God into a lie, and worshipped and served the creature more than the Creator, who is blessed for ever. Amen. For this cause God gave them up unto vile affections: for even their women did change the natural use into that which is against nature: And likewise also the men, leaving the natural use of the woman, burned in their lust one toward another; men with men working that which is unseemly, and receiving in themselves that recompence of their error which was meet. And even as they did not like to retain God in their knowledge, God gave them over to a reprobate mind, to do those things which are not convenient; Being filled with all unrighteousness, fornication, wickedness, covetousness, maliciousness; full of envy, murder, debate, deceit, malignity; whisperers, Backbiters, haters of God, despiteful, proud, boasters, inventors of evil things, disobedient to parents, Without understanding, covenantbreakers, without natural affection, implacable, unmerciful: Who knowing the judgment of God, that they which commit such things are worthy of death, not only do the same, but have pleasure in them that do them.*

Even though they knew the judgment of God and what happens to those who commit such things, they not only did them, but they took pleasure in those who did as well. And God gave them up to uncleanness and vile affections.

I pray these Scriptures will serve as a warning to us all. Sexual sin—and sin as a whole—is nothing to rejoice in. For so long, many of us knew the judgment of God and what happens to those who commit such things and yet, we chose to return to sexual sin again and again. We took pleasure in those who committed such acts as we were looking for *satisfaction* from them.

I pray you have seen why you should not remain in a state of sexual sin. May you find no pleasure in sexual immorality, nor those who commit such acts.

Pray for those who engage in sexual sin and provide such things for self-gratification. Many are trapped, bound, and lost. They too are in need of the love and grace of God. May our light expose this evil and not give it room to grow in the shadows of homes and within the hearts of men.

# Clean Slate

## DAY 11

Hebrews 11:1—*Now faith is the substance of things hoped for, the evidence of things not seen.*

Through faith, the men and women in Hebrews 11 were looking for entry into the eternal city.[150] The eternal city was the *substance* of what they were hoping for. The *evidence* of what they were hoping for was displayed through their actions. They lived as people who believed they would one day enter the eternal city—holy and righteous.

As you look upon this great cloud of witnesses thousands of years later,[151] I pray you will set your sights on the eternal city. May the evidence of your life reveal someone who is ready to enter the eternal city as well.

Part of your *evidence* is living a sexually pure life. Believe it can be yours by faith. Allow your actions to align with what you believe. No matter what happens, keep your sights on the eternal city and the evidence of a holy and righteous life before God.

---

[150] Hebrews 11:13–16.

[151] Hebrews 12:1–4.

## DAY 12

Hebrews 11:6—*But without faith it is impossible to please him: for he that cometh to God must believe that he is, and that he is a rewarder of them that diligently seek him.*

Many of us have struggled with sexual sin for so long that it was hard to believe we could ever live sexually pure. It was not that we did not want to please God—we did—but for one reason or another, our struggle slowly diminished any hope of freedom from sexual sin.

But here is the beauty and power of Hebrews 11:6. God is available to everyone. We can come to Him in our time of need.[152] And when you come to God in repentance, I want you to believe in who He is, what He has accomplished through His Son, what He will accomplish in the future, and what He can do in—and through—you. I want you to believe God is your redeemer, your strength, your provider, your defense, and your salvation.[153] He rewards everyone who diligently seeks Him.

God started a good work in you. His purpose is for you to be conformed into the image of His Son.[154] And God will see the good work He began in you to its completion.[155]

Let your faith in overcoming sexual sin be reignited. Please God through your faith. Allow His grace to help you in your weakness. Seek Him diligently through prayer, bible reading, and praise and worship. He will reward you.

---

[152] Hebrews 4:14–16.

[153] Psalm 18:2, 19:14, 103:1–12.

[154] Romans 8:28–29.

[155] Philippians 1:6.

DAY 13

Psalm 103:11–12—*The LORD is merciful and gracious, slow to anger, and plenteous in mercy. He will not always chide: neither will he keep his anger for ever. He hath not dealt with us after our sins; nor rewarded us according to our iniquities. For as the heaven is high above the earth, so great is his mercy toward them that fear him. As far as the east is from the west, so far hath he removed our transgressions from us.*

When thinking about having a clean slate, it is beautiful to know God is merciful and gracious. Consider how high heaven is above the earth. That is a lot of mercy God provides those who fear Him.

Those who fear God would be cautious of how they live before Him, not wanting to willfully disobey Him or act contrary to His word or will.

Along with His mercy, God removes our sins from us as far as the east is from the west. And as the east and west will not come together, our sins are removed from us in the same manner.

God is slow to anger and plenteous in mercy. He is giving us an opportunity to live a holy life unto Him.[156] May His mercy and forgiveness help us have the clean slate we have been looking for.

---

[156] 2 Peter 3:9.

## DAY 14

Matthew 6:14–15—*For if ye forgive men their trespasses, your heavenly Father will also forgive you: But if ye forgive not men their trespasses, neither will your Father forgive your trespasses.*

As we seek forgiveness from the Lord, we must first forgive those who sinned against us. Where we have been hurt and scarred by others, holding onto unforgiveness can keep us angry, ill-mannered, destructive toward others, and eternally separated from God.[157]

I pray you will seek the Lord to help you work through your hurt and unforgiveness. I pray you will allow Him to help you forgive those who wronged you so you can live in the freedom Jesus died to give you.

If you would like additional information on forgiveness, please review my book, *Forgive: Living Free from the Pain of Offense* on the Commission Publishing website.

---

[157] Revelation 21:8.

# DAY 15

1 John 3:18—*My little children, let us not love in word, neither in tongue; but in deed and in truth.*

Love is more than a feeling. Love is a commitment. And with this commitment, you will discover protection, support, giving, patience, kindness, honesty, sacrifice, and hope (among other things).

As you seek to love others, I want you to also commit to loving yourself—in deed and truth. Consider how you can place a greater emphasis on your physical, mental, and emotional well-being. Build support systems to keep you far from sexual sin. Exercise patient endurance so you can walk in sexual purity. Make the appropriate sacrifices for the good of your soul and your life before God. Live with integrity. And do not lose hope.

*May love be most evident in how you care for your life and others before God and your fellow man.*

## A Lost Love

DAY 16

Proverbs 8:13—*The fear of the LORD is to hate evil: pride, and arrogancy, and the evil way, and the froward mouth, do I hate.*

When we fear the Lord, we will hate four specific *areas* of evil: 1) pride, 2) arrogance, 3) the evil way, and the 4) froward (perverse) mouth. But when we do these things, we show that we love evil and do not fear God. Our actions show what is in our hearts.[158]

Fearing God goes beyond what we speak or the few good things we do for Him. Fearing God comes down to our actions —actions that make pride, arrogance, the evil way, and the froward mouth an enemy rather than a friend.

*Love God. Hate evil. Fear Him.*

---

[158] Matthew 15:10–20.

DAY 17

Proverbs 4:23—*Keep thy heart with all diligence; for out of it are the issues of life.*

When you keep your heart with all diligence, you are to guard it. A guard can be a man, post, or prison. Guards, posts, and prisons have specific purposes. They have a responsibility to protect what they are watching over from internal and external threats. They maintain accountability and surveillance to control and protect access. Guards implement specific protocols to preserve proper integrity.

Your heart is a priceless asset. It is the center of your thoughts and feelings. But like many of us, you might not have guarded your heart as if it was priceless.

*Have you considered internal and external threats?*

*Have you ensured your heart does not drift into dangerous areas of thought or desire?*

*What protocols have you established (bible reading, prayer, praise and worship, etc.) to keep your heart and life in the right areas?*

Your heart will not keep its way. It is deceitful above all things.[159] You must be vigilant and actively engaged to ensure your heart is adequately protected and built up in righteousness.[160]

---

[159] Jeremiah 17:9.

[160] Psalm 119:11.

## DAY 18

*Luke 14:25–33—And there went great multitudes with him: and he turned, and said unto them, If any man come to me, and hate not his father, and mother, and wife, and children, and brethren, and sisters, yea, and his own life also, he cannot be my disciple. And whosoever doth not bear his cross, and come after me, cannot be my disciple. For which of you, intending to build a tower, sitteth not down first, and counteth the cost, whether he have sufficient to finish it? Lest haply, after he hath laid the foundation, and is not able to finish it, all that behold it begin to mock him, Saying, This man began to build, and was not able to finish. Or what king, going to make war against another king, sitteth not down first, and consulteth whether he be able with ten thousand to meet him that cometh against him with twenty thousand? Or else, while the other is yet a great way off, he sendeth an ambassage, and desireth conditions of peace. So likewise, whosoever he be of you that forsaketh not all that he hath, he cannot be my disciple.*

Before the builder and king proceeded, they considered whether they could complete their *tasks* successfully. The builder was not going to start the project if he was not able to finish it. Likewise, the king would not go to war with an army half the size of another unless he knew he could overtake that army. The results for moving forward without considering the cost would have been devastating.

How many of us consider—or considered—whether we could live out your days as a faithful disciple? Sure, we want the benefits of heaven and blessings on earth but what about the other *things* that come with being a disciple? Persecution, loss, and forsaking everything we have and everything we ever wanted or wanted to be. We have to give it all up. But how many of us try to have it all. We want a good life and God. We want riches in earth and heaven. And we might become upset when we cannot have them.

Think about what happens when disciples do not finish their race or live up to the *standard* Jesus establishes. They are like unfinished houses where people mock them and God, bringing shame to Jesus.[161]

The *cost* of discipleship is to forsake all. Some of us might experience blessings on earth and others might not.[162] Becoming a disciple does not guarantee happiness, good health, wealth, or success in the world. But by forsaking all, we are promised an eternal life with God; a life of joy, peace, and serenity in His presence forever.[163] Consider the *cost* today.

---

[161] Hebrews 6:6.

[162] Hebrews 11:17–40.

[163] Revelation 21:1–4.

## DAY 19

John 14:23–24—*Jesus answered and said unto him, If a man love me, he will keep my words: and my Father will love him, and we will come unto him, and make our abode with him. He that loveth me not keepeth not my sayings: and the word which ye hear is not mine, but the Father's which sent me.*

If you will love Jesus and keep His words, three wonderful things will occur. The Father will 1) love you, 2) both Jesus and the Father will come to you, and 3) they will make their dwelling place with you. Jesus said those who keep His commandments would be given the Holy Spirit to abide with them forever.[164]

The word abode here is the same as *mansion*. As Jesus prepares a mansion for you in the kingdom of God, both He and the Father will make their residence with you on the earth.[165] They will be so pleased with your life that they will come to you and reside with you. *Amen!*

Let us desire to please the Father by loving Jesus and keeping His words.

---

[164] John 14:15–16.

[165] John 14:1–4.

## DAY 20

Matthew 5:14–16—*Ye are the light of the world. A city that is set on an hill cannot be hid. Neither do men light a candle, and put it under a bushel, but on a candlestick; and it giveth light unto all that are in the house. Let your light so shine before men, that they may see your good works, and glorify your Father which is in heaven.*

The purpose of the light we shine in the world is not to bring attention to ourselves. It is to bring glory to God.

Jesus does not mention specific talents or gifts that we must have or any unique skill—merely good works. *Good works* can be acts or deeds that are beautiful, virtuous, honest, or valuable. Many good works are accomplished without cost or in-depth biblical knowledge. But they do require conscious effort, focus, or purpose in wanting to do something *good*.

The good works we can do are meant for God to get the credit. They are for Him to receive honor and glory. It provides an opportunity for God to be acknowledged, shared, and known.

Look for ways to shine your light today. Take pleasure in God being glorified through the good works you accomplish.

## A City Under Attack

### DAY 21

Ephesians 4:27—*Neither give place to the devil.*

If you give the devil any place, he will try to destroy your life, but not before trying to take everything he can from you. Of all he wants to take from you, your good name is one of the most important. A good name is more desirable than riches.[166] And with your name destroyed, so is your testimony of Christ.

The devil will use people, the media (television, movies, radio, songs), and any other thing to tempt you. But he does not need a lot of *room* to operate with, just a small *place.*

Be sober-minded and vigilant. Guard yourself against the onslaught of the enemy. One curious look. One turn of a television channel. One search on the Internet. All these things can lead to giving a *place* to the devil.

Stay clear of temptation and curiosity. Give your *all* to God and nothing to the devil.

---

[166] Proverbs 22:1.

DAY 22

James 5:16—*Confess your faults one to another, and pray one for another, that ye may be healed. The effectual fervent prayer of a righteous man availeth much.*

Though many people struggle with sexual sin, we often isolate ourselves in the shadows of despair. Pride, fear, shame, and guilt keep us from coming into the light to seek help and support.

It takes courage to ask for help and confess your faults to another person. And I applaud you for taking these steps to come into the light. Having a safe *place* to confess your faults can feel like heavy weights being lifted from your shoulders. Just knowing you no longer have to carry your burdens alone can bring the hope of healing, restoration, and peace.[167]

As the effectual fervent prayer of a righteous man avails much, I pray you will find people like this who will help you, fervently pray for you, and encourage you to abstain from sin.

---

[167] Galatians 6:1–2.

## DAY 23

Hebrews 12:5–14—*And ye have forgotten the exhortation which speaketh unto you as unto children, My son, despise not thou the chastening of the Lord, nor faint when thou art rebuked of him: For whom the Lord loveth he chasteneth, and scourgeth every son whom he receiveth. If ye endure chastening, God dealeth with you as with sons; for what son is he whom the father chasteneth not? But if ye be without chastisement, whereof all are partakers, then are ye bastards, and not sons. Furthermore we have had fathers of our flesh which corrected us, and we gave themreverence: shall we not much rather be in subjection unto the Father of spirits, and live? For they verily for a few days chastened us after their own pleasure; but he for ourprofit, that we might be partakers of his holiness. Now no chastening for the present seemeth to be joyous, but grievous: nevertheless afterward it yieldeth the peaceable fruit of righteousness unto them which are exercised thereby. Wherefore lift up the hands which hang down, and the feeble knees; And make straight paths for your feet, lest that which is lame be turned out of the way; but let it rather be healed. Follow peace with all men, and holiness, without which no man shall see the Lord:*

When the Lord loves us, He chastises us. He wants us to yield the peaceable fruit of righteousness and follow peace and holiness.

Let us thank God for His love and chastising. Though it does not feel good while we are going through it, the benefits far exceed where we would have been had the Lord not intervened. *God wants to see us!*

# DAY 24

John 15:1–8—*I am the true vine, and my Father is the husbandman. Every branch in me that beareth not fruit he taketh away: and every branch that beareth fruit, he purgeth it, that it may bring forth more fruit. Now ye are clean through the word which I have spoken unto you. Abide in me, and I in you. As the branch cannot bear fruit of itself, except it abide in the vine; no more can ye, except ye abide in me. I am the vine, ye are the branches: He that abideth in me, and I in him, the same bringeth forth much fruit: for without me ye can do nothing. If a man abide not in me, he is cast forth as a branch, and is withered; and men gather them, and cast them into the fire, and they are burned. If ye abide in me, and my words abide in you, ye shall ask what ye will, and it shall be done unto you. Herein is my Father glorified, that ye bear much fruit; so shall ye be my disciples.*

Like those God chastises, He prunes those who bear good fruit. He does this so they can bear even more fruit.

But we should never think we can reach a point where we can bear fruit on our own, in our strength. We can only bring forth fruit by remaining in Him.

Let us glorify our Father in heaven by bearing much fruit. Abide in Jesus and allow Him to shape and mold you to reflect His image and character in the world.

The fruit you bear can benefit many people. Consider ways you can help and encourage someone close to you, especially someone who might be struggling with sexual sin.

## DAY 25

Galatians 5:15–25—*This I say then, Walk in the Spirit, and ye shall not fulfil the lust of the flesh. For the flesh lusteth against the Spirit, and the Spirit against the flesh: and these are contrary the one to the other: so that ye cannot do the things that ye would. But if ye be led of the Spirit, ye are not under the law. Now the works of the flesh are manifest, which are these; Adultery, fornication, uncleanness, lasciviousness, Idolatry, witchcraft, hatred, variance, emulations, wrath, strife, seditions, heresies, Envyings, murders, drunkenness, revellings, and such like: of the which I tell you before, as I have also told you in time past, that they which do such things shall not inherit the kingdom of God. But the fruit of the Spirit is love, joy, peace, longsuffering, gentleness, goodness, faith, Meekness, temperance: against such there is no law. And they that are Christ's have crucified the flesh with the affections and lusts. If we live in the Spirit, let us also walk in the Spirit.*

The fruit of the Spirit are characteristics borne to those who live, walk, and are led by the Spirit. When you live, walk, and are led by the Spirit, you crucify the flesh along with its affections and lusts. This encompasses a way of life and a way to think, engage, and interact with the world around you. Take several moments to meditate on the fruit of the Spirit, and choose to live, walk, and be led by the Spirit.

# Bodybuilding

## DAY 26

Psalm 101:3—*I will set no wicked thing before mine eyes: I hate the work of them that turn aside; it shall not cleave to me.*

What a declaration David made in not wanting to set any wicked thing before his eyes. He made an intentional commitment to live in integrity; to hate the work of those who turn from what is right, and not allow it to cleave to him.

I pray you will make a similar declaration as David. May you make an intentional commitment not to set any wicked thing before your eyes. This might require you to stop watching television or going to specific locations.

In the area of sexual sin, I pray you will hate the work of those who produce and engage in pornographic productions and other sexually illicit activities. But pray for their deliverance so they might find the same freedom, peace, and salvation through Christ as you have.

Lastly, I pray you will not allow sexual sin to cleave to you. Make the intentional decision to stay clear of it and remove it far from your eyes and life.

## DAY 27

Romans 12:1—*I beseech you therefore, brethren, by the mercies of God, that ye present your bodies a living sacrifice, holy, acceptable unto God, which is your reasonable service.*

One of the definitions of *sacrifice* is the surrender or destruction of something prized or desirable for the sake of something considered as having a higher or more important value or claim. But unlike sacrifices whose lives are ended to benefit another, living sacrifices surrender the desires and appetites of their flesh to live holy and acceptable unto God each day. *This is their reasonable service.*

As we live before God, let us present ourselves as living sacrifices. Let us give up those desires and appetites that keep us in sin and darkness. May a holy and acceptable lifestyle become our reasonable service unto Him.

DAY 28

Romans 10:17—So then faith cometh by hearing, and hearing by the word of God.

*Where were you when you first believed in Jesus?*

I was in Alaska on a military assignment in March 1997. I was invited to a local church where I heard a preacher talk about Jesus and being connected to the power source—*and I wanted to be connected.* Hearing the word of God through the pastor's sermon changed my life forever.

Take a few moments to reflect on your first instances of faith in Christ. God began a good work in you on that day.[168] And no matter what you have been through thus far, believe He will see His good work in you to its completion.

Faith is not about what *is*, it is believing what *will be* through Jesus Christ.

---

[168] Philippians 1:6.

## DAY 29

Psalm 19:14—*Let the words of my mouth, and the meditation of my heart, be acceptable in thy sight, O LORD, my strength, and my redeemer.*

*Consider what you have said and meditated on in the last twenty-four hours. Would they be acceptable to God?*

As we seek to live holy and acceptable lives unto God, let us be very careful about what we say and meditate upon. Sometimes we might become careless about what we say or meditate on things that are not godly. We allow ourselves to become more focused on our desires and appetites rather than pleasing God. But no matter the occasion, we must remember to set our intentions on pleasing God at all times—even in the secret places of our heart.

David described the Lord as His strength and redeemer. As He can save you from every test, trial, and struggle, trust Him to strengthen you in your weak areas. Stay mindful of Him, so your words and meditations can lead to righteous acts in His sight.

DAY 30

Proverbs 5:3–13—*For the lips of a strange woman drop as an honeycomb, and her mouth is smoother than oil: But her end is bitter as wormwood, sharp as a twoedged sword. Her feet go down to death; her steps take hold on hell. Lest thou shouldest ponder the path of life, her ways are moveable, that thou canst not know them. Hear me now therefore, O ye children, and depart not from the words of my mouth. Remove thy way far from her, and come not nigh the door of her house: Lest thou give thine honour unto others, and thy years unto the cruel: Lest strangers be filled with thy wealth; and thy labours be in the house of a stranger; And thou mourn at the last, when thy flesh and thy body are consumed, And say, How have I hated instruction, and my heart despised reproof; And have not obeyed the voice of my teachers, nor inclined mine ear to them that instructed me!*

*How many times have you remained near the door of those who sexually tempted you?*

The longer you stay around, the chances keep increasing that you will come closer to the *door*, and walk into the house. But to keep yourself clear of these dangers, you must decide to stay far from them. You cannot allow anyone to believe you are interested in sexually illicit activities. You must intentionally stay far from them and even build a plan to keep yourself free from their calls of temptation.

## Military Support

### DAY 31

Hebrews 5:11–14—*Of whom we have many things to say, and hard to be uttered, seeing ye are dull of hearing. For when for the time ye ought to be teachers, ye have need that one teach you again which be the first principles of the oracles of God; and are become such as have need of milk, and not of strong meat. For every one that useth milk is unskilful in the word of righteousness: for he is a babe. But strong meat belongeth to them that are of full age, even those who by reason of use have their senses exercised to discern both good and evil.*

There are many things we can learn about the word of God. The word of God is powerful. It is living and active;[169] it can keep you from sin;[170] and it provides doctrine, reproof, correction, and instruction in righteousness to make you perfect and thoroughly furnished unto all good works.[171]

It is not enough to have the word of God on your phone or in your home. Without reading, studying, meditating, and applying the word of God, you will remain unskilled in the word of righteousness. You will have to continue learning the same subjects again and again.

Each of us can grow in our knowledge of the word of God, and it begins with exercising our senses through its use. Take time each day to interact with the word of God.

---

[169] Hebrews 4:12.

[170] Psalm 119:11.

[171] 2 Timothy 3:16–17.

DAY 32

Ephesians 4:29—*Let no corrupt communication proceed out of your mouth, but that which is good to the use of edifying, that it may minister grace unto the hearers.*

Corrupt communication is bad, rotten, and worthless to ourselves and others. As Paul encourages the Ephesians, we should allow our conversations to be good, edifying, and minister grace to our hearers.

In the area of sexual sin, I would like to encourage you to share your journey of sexual addiction and sexual purity with one person or group. As no temptation is uncommon to man, many people around you might be struggling to find help.

Be discerning and ask the Lord to show you when, where, and with whom to share your message of courage and freedom. You never know the impact your story might have on another person or group. You might be the encouragement someone needs to take a personal stand against sexual addiction and sin.

## DAY 33

*Isaiah 52:7—How beautiful upon the mountains are the feet of him that bringeth good tidings, that publisheth peace; that bringeth good tidings of good, that publisheth salvation; that saith unto Zion, Thy God reigneth!*

We all like to receive good news. How blessed are we when those who are peaceful, happy in the Lord, and speak truth come around us. They often call us when we most need a word of encouragement and provide hope when life seems hopeless.

Today, I want to encourage you to be such a person. There are people around you who are depressed, stressed, and bound by sin. Let your presence and your words be such that it encourages and helps them keep their focus on the Lord.

The next time someone you know comes to mind, say a prayer for him or her, and reach out by calling or stopping by for a visit. Sometimes your presence and encouragement might be what someone needs to continue in his or her walk with the Lord.

DAY 34

1 Corinthians 16:13—*Watch ye, stand fast in the faith, quit you like men, be strong.*

As Paul was providing his final comments to the church in Corinth in his first letter, he tells them four things. May these areas be found in your life and walk with God:

*1. Be on their guard (watch ye).* If you are on your guard, you are watchful for anything or anyone in and out of its proper place (e.g., people, doctrine, etc.). Discern good and evil. Pray continually.

*2. Stand firm in the faith.* Stand firm in your belief in God and the gift of eternal life. Do not allow anyone or anything move you from your stance of faithful obedience to God's word and will and the hope you have in Him as your provider, protector, and salvation.

*3. Act like mature men (quit you like men).* When you think about acting like a man, you might think of attributes such as responsible, truthful, accountable, industrious, protector, teacher, and provider. These are attributes others should see in disciples of Jesus.

*4. Be strong.* Be strong in the Lord and in the power of His might.[172] As you serve and minister, do so in the strength God supplies so that in everything you do or say, God is glorified through Jesus Christ.[173]

---

[172] Ephesians 6:10.

[173] Matthew 5:14–16; 1 Peter 4:11.

## DAY 35

*James 1:12—Blessed is the man that endureth temptation: for when he is tried, he shall receive the crown of life, which the Lord hath promised to them that love him.*

Blessed is the man that endures temptation. To endure is to have fortitude and perseverance. Living a life of sexual purity does not mean temptations will never come. They will. But it does mean we can have the perseverance and fortitude not to give into them.

When I first found restoration and freedom from sexual sin, I thought I would never be sexually tempted again. But when sexual temptation returned, I did not apply what I previously learned. I became *shell-shocked* by what was going on. I soon allowed the temptation to speak to me as it had before, and not long after, I gave into sexual sin once again.

Being tempted is not a sin, giving into the temptation is.[174] At some point, you might be tried, but using the tools and resources you have learned throughout this book can help you remain as a faithful disciple of Jesus.

Remember, blessed are you when you endure temptation. Live a faithful life unto God, day-by-day, and moment-by-moment. May you keep your hope set on the crown of life that is given to all who love Him, those who are tested and overcome.

*Live in the freedom Christ died to give you.*

*Be vigilant. Be watchful.*

*Stand.*

---

174 Matthew 4:1–11; Hebrews 4:15.

(com)mission
PUBLISHING

www.commissionpubs.com
info@commissionpubs.com

www.ingramcontent.com/pod-product-compliance
Lightning Source LLC
Chambersburg PA
CBHW071903020426
42331CB00010B/2649